T0342775

The Pizza Patch

by

Jill McDougall

photography by

Lindsay Edwards

OXFORD
UNIVERSITY PRESS
AUSTRALIA & NEW ZEALAND

OXFORD
UNIVERSITY PRESS

Oxford University Press is a department of the University of Oxford.
It furthers the University's objective of excellence in research,
scholarship, and education by publishing worldwide. Oxford is a registered
trademark of Oxford University Press in the UK and in certain other countries.

Published in Australia by
Oxford University Press
Level 8, 737 Bourke Street, Docklands, Victoria 3008, Australia

Text © Jill McDougall 2014, 2019

The moral rights of the author have been asserted

First published 2014
This edition 2019
Reprinted 2021

ISBN 9780190317652

Photography by Lindsay Edwards
Illustrations by Agnese Baruzzi
Printed in Singapore by Markono Print Media Pte Ltd

*Links to third party websites are provided by Oxford in good faith and for information only.
Oxford disclaims any responsibility for the materials contained in any third party website
referenced in this work.*

Acknowledgements

Series Editor: Nikki Gamble

The publishers would like to thank the following for the permission to
reproduce photographs:

Background images by Aksenenko Olga/Shutterstock; Primopiano/Shutterstock;
Chieferu/iStockphoto; Elena Kalistratova/Shutterstock; Picsfive/Shutterstock;
Tratong/Shutterstock; Brandon Bourdages/Shutterstock; DenisNata/Shutterstock;
Johann Helgason/Shutterstock.

Cover photograph by Lindsay Edwards;
cover background: Primopiano/Shutterstock

We have made every effort to trace and contact all copyright holders before
publication. If notified, the publisher will rectify any errors or omissions at the
earliest opportunity.

With thanks to Marcus, Emily and everyone in class 2D.

Contents

The Best Spot

by CHARLOTTE

Today is cool and cloudy.

We're going to build a food garden at school. Today, Mrs Lee helped us to plan it.

This spot looks good!

Mrs Lee knows everything about gardening.

First, we found the best place for our garden. It's a sunny spot that's sheltered from the wind. It's close to a water tap, and Mrs Lee says it has really good soil, too.

If we plan our garden well, hopefully we will grow lots of food.

OUR GARDEN PLAN

garden beds

fruit trees

compost bins

worm farm

chicken coop

Watch Out Weeds!

by <u>KEVIN</u>

Today is hot and windy.

Today, everyone helped build the garden. Gemma and I dug up **weeds** and put them in a bucket of water. In a few weeks, we will take the rotting weeds out of the water and put them in the **compost** bin.

Watch out weeds!

We don't stand a chance!

6

Our new garden is ready for planting!

The Pizza Patch

by STELLA

Today is bright and sunny.

Today, we made a pizza patch – we really did! A pizza patch grows veggies and herbs to go on pizzas.

TIPS FOR MAKING A PIZZA PATCH

1. Pull the weeds out of your garden bed and rake the soil.

2. Add some **manure**.

3. Add some straw to keep the soil from getting dry.

4. Plant different **seedlings** in different parts of the garden bed. Each plant will grow a topping for a pizza.

We are growing tomatoes, spring onions, zucchinis and basil for our pizzas.

Josh and I are planting a tomato seedling.

A Lot of Rot

by ZOE
★ ★ ★

Today is hot and dry.

Today, we made compost. Compost is made from lots of things that rot. It's a great **fertiliser** for plants.

Emily and I are putting some leaves into the compost bin.

COMPOST RECIPE

You will need:

- green stuff (fresh grass and plant clippings)

- brown stuff (dried leaves and straw)

- fruit and vegetable scraps

- a handful of soil

- water.

What to do:

- Put the green stuff, brown stuff, scraps and soil into your compost bin.

- Then sprinkle on some water until the pile is damp.

- Over time, everything will rot and ... guess what! You've made compost!

From Flower to Fruit

by _ALEX_

Today is warm.

Big yellow flowers are growing on the zucchini plant. Behind them, baby zucchinis are starting to grow!

1 Flowers grow on the plant.

2 Bees move **pollen** from one flower to another.

3 Tiny zucchinis start to grow.

The Worm Farm

by MARCUS

Today is windy.

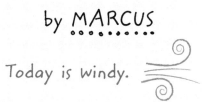
Worms are cool.

Today, we looked at our worm farm. The worms munch on food scraps and leave behind heaps of worm poo (called castings).

We mixed some worm poo with water to make a kind of worm tea. We fed this to the plants.

Our worm tea will help the plants grow.

Eww, worm poo!

14

THE WORM FARM

Chomp! Chomp!

straw

food scraps

lots of worms

TODAY'S MENU

teabags

apple cores

MENU

eggshells

worm castings

water that drips out

Pesky Pests

by *VANESSA*

Today is showery.

Help! The pizza patch is being invaded! It's not aliens invading our garden, it's pests. Snails are snacking on the basil and slugs are chomping on the tomatoes.

We picked off the pests and fed them to the chickens.

Gulp!

GOT YOU!

We catch snails and slugs with old orange halves. They creep under them to hide from the sun.

BUGS THAT EAT OTHER BUGS

Not all bugs in the garden are pests. These bugs feed on the pesky plant-eaters.

ladybird

lacewing

hover fly

ground beetle

The Scarecrow

by ANDY

Today is sunny.

Some of the cherry tomatoes are ripe. I popped one in my mouth and splat – it burst open! It was warm and sweet – *yum*!

Birds like to eat tomatoes, too. We had to come up with a plan to scare them away, so we made a **scarecrow**!

Scarecrows can keep birds away.

Time to Pick!

by *GEORGE*

Today is warm.

Hooray – the pizza plants are ready for picking! Tomorrow we'll have a pizza party!

Today we picked:

- tomatoes
- zucchinis
- basil leaves
- spring onions.

The Pizza Party

by CHARLOTTE

Today is bright and sunny.

Today the school kitchen was a busy place. We made pizza dough and chopped up lots of veggies. Soon we could smell pizzas cooking!

My pizza had cheese, zucchini, tomato, basil and spring onion. I was about to pick up a slice when ... oops! A hungry caterpillar had crawled onto my pizza!

Glossary

compost: rotted plant and food waste that is used to feed living plants

fertiliser: food for plants

manure: poo from animals such as cows, horses and chickens

pollen: a powder made by flowers

scarecrow: something that looks like a person and is put in a garden to scare birds away

seedlings: young plants grown from seed

weeds: plants that grow where you don't want them

Index